MacKinnon

by Stephen Aldhouse

D0417930

Lang**Syne**

PUBLISHING

WRITING *to* REMEMBER

Lang**Syne**

PUBLISHING

WRITING *to* REMEMBER

Vineyard Business Centre,
Pathhead, Midlothian EH37 5XP
Tel: 01875 321 203 Fax: 01875 321 233
E-mail: info@lang-syne.co.uk
www.langsyneshop.co.uk

Design by Dorothy Meikle
Printed by Montgomery Litho, Glasgow
© Lang Syne Publishers Ltd 2011

ISBN 978-1-85217-074-5

MacKinnon

SEPT NAMES INCLUDE:

Love
MacKinney
MacKinning
MacKinven
MacMorran

MacKinnon

MOTTO:
Audentes fortuna juvat
(Fortune assists the daring).

CREST:
A Silver Boar's Head
with the Shank Bone of a Deer
in its Mouth Proper.

TERRITORY:
Principally Strathardale, or Strathaird,
to Broadford and Kyleakin in Skye,
and Mishnish in Mull.
Also in Arran, Kintyre and Tiree.
Mostly lost in the 18th century.

Chapter one:

The origins of the clan system

by Rennie McOwan

The original Scottish clans of the Highlands and the great families of the Lowlands and Borders were gatherings of families, relatives, allies and neighbours for mutual protection against rivals or invaders.

Scotland experienced invasion from the Vikings, the Romans and English armies from the south. The Norman invasion of what is now England also had an influence on land-holding in Scotland. Some of these invaders stayed on and in time became 'Scottish'.

The word clan derives from the Gaelic language term 'clann', meaning children, and it was first used many centuries ago as communities were formed around tribal lands in glens and mountain fastnesses.

The format of clans changed over the centuries, but at its best the chief and his family held the land on behalf of all, like trustees, and the ordinary clansmen and women believed they had a blood relationship with the founder of their clan.

There were two way duties and obligations. An inadequate chief could be deposed and replaced by someone of greater ability.

Clan people had an immense pride in race. Their relationship with the chief was like adult children to a father and they had a real dignity.

The concept of clanship is very old and a more feudal notion of authority gradually crept in.

Pictland, for instance, was divided into seven principalities ruled by feudal leaders who were the strongest and most charismatic leaders of their particular groups.

By the sixth century the 'British' kingdoms of Strathclyde, Lothian and Celtic Dalriada (Argyll) had emerged and Scotland, as one nation, began to take shape in the time of King Kenneth MacAlpin.

Some chiefs claimed descent from

ancient kings which may not have been accurate in every case.

By the twelfth and thirteenth centuries the clans and families were more strongly brought under the central control of Scottish monarchs.

Lands were awarded and administered more and more under royal favour, yet the power of the area clan chiefs was still very great.

The long wars to ensure Scotland's independence against the expansionist ideas of English monarchs extended the influence of some clans and reduced the lands of others.

Those who supported Scotland's greatest king, Robert the Bruce, were awarded the territories of the families who had opposed his claim to the Scottish throne.

In the Scottish Borders country - the notorious Debatable Lands - the great families built up a ferocious reputation for providing war-like men accustomed to raiding into England and occasionally fighting one another.

Chiefs had the power to dispense justice

and to confiscate lands and clan warfare produced a society where martial virtues - courage, hardiness, tenacity - were greatly admired.

Gradually the relationship between the clans and the Crown became strained as Scottish monarchs became more orientated to life in the Lowlands and, on occasion, towards England.

The Highland clans spoke a different language, Gaelic, whereas the language of Lowland Scotland and the court was Scots and in more modern times, English.

Highlanders dressed differently, had different customs, and their wild mountain land sometimes seemed almost foreign to people living in the Lowlands.

It must be emphasised that Gaelic culture was very rich and story-telling, poetry, piping, the clarsach (harp) and other music all flourished and were greatly respected.

Highland culture was different from other parts of Scotland but it was not inferior or less sophisticated.

Central Government, whether in London

"The spirit of the clan means much to thousands of people"

or Edinburgh, sometimes saw the Gaelic clans as a challenge to their authority and some sent expeditions into the Highlands and west to crush the power of the Lords of the Isles.

Nevertheless, when the eighteenth century Jacobite Risings came along the cause of the Stuarts was mainly supported by Highland clans.

The word Jacobite comes from the Latin for James - Jacobus. The Jacobites wanted to restore the exiled Stuarts to the throne of Britain.

The monarchies of Scotland and England became one in 1603 when King James VI of Scotland (1st of England) gained the English throne after Queen Elizabeth died.

The Union of Parliaments of Scotland and England, the Treaty of Union, took place in 1707.

Some Highland clans, of course, and Lowland families opposed the Jacobites and supported the incoming Hanoverians.

After the Jacobite cause finally went down at Culloden in 1746 a kind of ethnic cleansing took place. The power of the chiefs was curtailed. Tartan and the pipes were banned in law.

Many emigrated, some because they wanted to, some because they were evicted by force. In addition, many Highlanders left for the cities of the south to seek work.

Many of the clan lands became home to sheep and deer shooting estates.

But the warlike traditions of the clans and the great Lowland and Border families lived on, with their descendants fighting bravely for freedom in two world wars.

Remember the men from whence you came, says the Gaelic proverb, and to that could be added the role of many heroic women.

The spirit of the clan, of having roots, whether Highland or Lowland, means much to thousands of people.

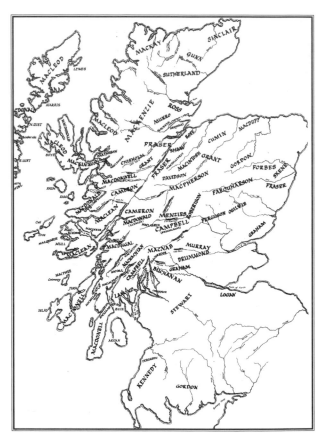

A map of the clans' homelands

Chapter two:

The western mists

Tradition traces the Clan MacKinnon back to Fingon (the fair-born) but when and where did he live? Possibly in Arran, Kintyre or Mull. He is said to have been the grandson of Gregor and the great-grandson of Kenneth MacAlpin, but there is no documentary evidence.

Another history places Gregor as one of King Alpin's sons, younger brother to Kenneth MacAlpin and Donald, and describes Findanus, Gregor's grandson, as the progenitor of the Clan MacKinnon, 'sons of Fingon of Findanus'. This puts Fingon at least four generations after King Alpin, who died in battle in 839 AD.

John Prebble, the noted historian and writer, mentions Grigor only in passing, as 'joint usurper with Eocha' in 878-89. The Edinburgh History gives the crown in these years to Eochaid, jointly with Giric, who was Donald's son and therefore Kenneth MacAlpin's nephew. We must

assume that Giric is another version of the name
Gregor. Neither mentions Fingon nor Findanus.

Kenneth MacAlpin was succeeded first
by his brother Donald and then by his sons
Constantine and Aodh. It was by killing Aodh that
Gregor obtained the crown. After Gregor's death
at Dundurn in Perthshire, the crown passed back
and forth between the descendants of Constantine
and Aodh for four generations.

Gregor's family were not included in
this arrangement and it may have been prudent
for them to withdraw westward, to Arran and
Kintyre, then northwards to Mull, and ally themselves to Norse settlers in the Isles.

Such an alliance is indicated by the tradition that Findanus, who had land on Mull,
acquired Dun Haakon (later Dunakin and now
Castle Maiol) by marriage to a Norse princess
around 900. If Findanus was the grandson of
Gregor, he would have been in his prime, say, 50
years after Gregor's rule, ie about 930, which is
reasonable agreement. Fingon may have been
another version of the name Findanus, or his son.

There was an Abbot of Iona called Fingon in 966, which would be about right for Findanus's son.

Dun Haakon was a broch, a round, double walled dry-stone tower, on the coast of Skye over-looking the 600m wide entrance to Loch Alsh. Tolls were levied on passing shipping, enforced by a chain, or, more likely, a boom of tree-trunks connected by chains, across the narrows.

Chapter three:

The prosperous years

There were MacKinnons on Arran in the early 14th century, for they and the MacDonalds welcomed Robert the Bruce while he was a fugitive from the kinsmen of the murdered Comyn and the forces of Edward I of England. After the death of Edward I, Bruce defeated Edward II at Bannockburn in 1314, where MacDonalds, and almost certainly MacKinnons with them, served in Bruce's own division. In reward, the MacKinnons received land in Strathardale on Skye (now Strathaird) and the castle of Dun Ringill. The clan prospered there until 1745, and the chiefs styled themselves 'of Strathardale'.

The MacKinnons still held land in Mishnish, the northernmost tip of Mull. There is also a 'MacKinnon's Cave' further south in Mull, at the foot of Glen Seilisdeir. The holdings of Ewan MacKinnon in Mishnish and

Strathardle were later confirmed by charter of James V, in 1542.

Fingal, the Gaelic warrior god, is said to have dined at the large block of stone at the entrance to MacKinnon's Cave. The cave turns sharply after a short distance so that the depths cannot be seen and are totally dark.

The tale is told on Mull that some local people wanted to know how far it ran. They sent in a piper, thinking that the sound of the pipes would come to the surface through fissures in the rock, and they could trace its extent. But the piper was attacked by the resident banshee and, although he piped boldly as he retreated, the banshee overcame him. His dog escaped, less most of its hair.

Branches of the clan held various offices by heredity, such as Master of the Household to the Lord of the Isles and custodians of standard weights and measures, Standard Bearer to the MacDonalds of Sleat, or Abbot of Iona. A hereditary abbacy seems strange to us, but could then occur in several ways. Celibacy was not so rigorously observed, nor was Inheritance necessarily by direct descent. Like the Crown, Inheritances may have passed by arrangement to nephews or other close relations. Also, some abbacies were laicised, that is, held for profit or prestige by someone not in holy orders. One Abbot of Iona, also named Fingon, and his brother Neil, were involved in a rebellion against the Lord of the Isles. This failed, and Neil was put to death. John MacKinnon was the last of the clan to be Abbot of Iona. In 1510, James IV petitioned the Pope to transfer the abbacy to George Hepburn, his favoured Bishop of the Isles.

The MacKinnons were normally loyal to the MacDonalds and the MacLeods; most disputes were against the MacLeans. In one incident, it is said that MacLeans seized some MacKinnon land in Mull while the chief was on Skye. On his return, the MacKinnons pursued them to their hall at Ledaig on the mainland, only to find them snoring drunkenly. Perhaps seeking to end, rather than exacerbate the feud, MacKinnon had his men cut fir trees, the clan badge, and plant them all

round the hall. To emphasize the point, he left a
naked sword against the tree before the door. The
MacLeans took the hint.

The MacKinnons of Strathardle occasionally found it expeditious to enter into formal
alliances with other clans. There are bonds of
manrent with MacNab of Bowaine in 1606 and
with MacGregor of MacGregor in 1671 Manrent
meant exactly what it says; the parties could call
upon each other in person for assistance.

For example, the wording of a bond
between Lord Kennedy, Sir Alexander Boyd and
Lord Fleming says that they and their *'kyn,
friendis and men'* would band together *'in all
thair caussis and querell, leifull and honest,
aganis al maner of persones, thair allegiance til
our soveran lord alanerly outan'* (the only exception).

The king probably insisted on the last
phrase, and in some circumstances prohibited
such alliances, suspecting conspiracy, no doubt.
Bonds of manrent were particularly popular in
uncertain times, such as during the minority of a
young successor to the throne.

The clans of the Isles valued their independence, and were prepared to pledge themselves to the Lord of the Isles in defending it. In Loch Finlaggan on Islay are two islands, on one of which the Lords of the Isles were ceremonially proclaimed. The other was known as the 'Isle of Counsel', and here the Lord and chiefs, including those of MacKinnon, met, together with the Bishop of the Isles and the Abbot of Iona (depending on the allegiance of those worthies). Their independence was maintained by juggling the balance of power between the Scottish kings, rival clans, the Norse, and sometimes the English. The Scottish kings, unable to control the highlands and islands, had to delegate their authority to local barons; when these became over-ambitious, or the king's hand too heavy, swords were drawn.

James IV, exasperated by the depredations, of the Islesmen, annexed the Isles (on paper, at least) in 1493. The opportunity to turn the tables came in 1545, when the Earl of Hertford was terrorising the Borders in an attempt to force the betrothal of the three-year-old Mary Queen of

Scots to Edward, son of Henry VIII of England.
The clans of the Isles, including MacKinnon of
Strathardle, were prepared to join the disaffected
Matthew Stewart, Earl of Lennox, whom Henry
had rather prematurely appointed Governor of
Scotland, in an insurrection.

This insurrection was rather ineffectual,
and by the turn of the century James IV was
attempting to subdue the Isles again. In 1608 his
envoys, Lord Ochiltree and Bishop Andrew
Knox, induced the chiefs, including Lachlan
MacKinnon of the Ilk, to board their ship in the
Sound of Mull. They were then seized and impris-
oned. Bishop Knox met these chiefs again the
following year on Iona, when they pledged themselves to the 'Statutes of Icolmkill (or Iona)'.
These were partly strategic arms limitation; the
size of the chief's retinue was limited; firearms
were prohibited; bards (and their rousing tales of
glory) were suppressed. There were also civil
matters concerning the church, inns and alcohol
control.

Chapter four:

Years of bloodshed

The inevitable collision between Scottish Presbyterianism and the high Episcopalianism imposed by Charles I came to a head in the signing of the Covenant by nobles and commoners alike. But this movement soon assumed a zealous bigotry and anti-royalism which was not intended in the original. Partly because of this, and partly because it was an Edinburgh and lowland-based movement supported by and benefiting the already over-powerful Campbells, the MacKinnons and other Islesmen were ready to support the king.

Although the chief, Lachlan Mor, was in the custody of Archibald Campbell, 8th Earl of Argyll, the MacKinnons joined James Graham, Marquis of Montrose, in his guerilla war. They were with him at the Battle of Inverlochy in 1645, more famous for the forced march that preceded it than Montrose's victory. Argyll had trapped

Montrose in the Great Glen between his army and another at Inverness, but Montrose marched his men for 30 miles, up Glen Tarff, to 2,500 feet over Carn Leac, through blizzards and waist-high snowdrifts and so down Glen Roy and the River Spean to outflank Argyll.

The execution of Charles I changed the heart of the Scots, and Argyll revised his plans. He not only became Royalist; he personally crowned Charles II at Scone, having first disposed of Montrose. He released Lachlan Mor, who raised a regiment to join Charles to march south into the trap laid by Cromwell, who defeated the Royalists at Worcester in 1651. Charles just had time to create Lachlan a knight banneret before leaving for France.

150 MacKinnons under Ian Dubh, the 29th chief, joined the Earl of Mar at the Battle of Sherrifmuir in the attempt, in 1715, to place James Stuart on the throne. When the rising failed, the clan lands were forfeit by the Act of Attainder. What followed was a remarkable story of high-land comradeship. The chief of Clan Grant, who

had not personally joined the rising, bought the MacKinnon lands and resold them to a MacKinnon clansman, who passed them on to Iain Dubh's heirs.

Undismayed, Iain Dubh and some 200 MacKinnons joined Prince Charles at Edinburgh in 1745, and were with him throughout the rising. He survived Culloden, and did what he could to rally the clans in the days following the battle. His own clan, however, had mostly gone away with the Earl of Cromarty, hoping to recover some of Prince Charles's treasury.

After his flight to Skye disguised as Flora MacDonald's maidservant, the Prince asked to go to the MacKinnons in Strathaird. With Malcolm MacLeod, and disguised as his servant, he walked from Portree to the house of Captain John MacKinnon in the village of Elgol on Strathaird. John, who was Iain Dubh's nephew, was out. On his return, he found the Prince carrying his baby son Neil round the room and singing to him. John was overcome with emotion and wept.

The MacKinnons sheltered the Prince in a

cave on the extreme southern tip of the Strathaird peninsula for a while. Then Iain Dubh, despite his 70 years of age, dodged two Government ships to take the Prince to Mallaig in his galley, but was captured on the voyage home. He and John had fallen into the hands of the notorious Captain Fergusson of *HMS Furnace*. Fergusson was described by a contemporary as *'of furious, savage disposition'*, and he and Captain Caroline Scott of Guise's Regiment, whose foul atrocities took no account of humanity or law, were at this time engaged in despoiling Barra and Mull, including the MacKinnon lands there.

Spuring the £30,000 reward and enduring a flogging, Iain Dubh refused to betray the Prince. He was kept in a prison ship at Tilbury, on the River Thames, then spent 18 months in the Tower of London. Late in 1747 he was tried, but pardoned because of his age and his *'mistaken sense of chivalry'*, and went home to Kilmorie, close by the now derelict Dun Ringill. His nephew John also returned to Skye, in the company of Flora MacDonald.

Iain Dubh's second wife died in 1753; his son was already dead. At 71, he married again and fathered two more boys and a girl. His son, Charles, had to part with the clan lands. His grandson, John, the last of this line, died unmarried in 1808.

Chapter five:

Clearances

There was a MacKinnon laird at Corrichatachan (now Corry) on Broadford Bay in Skye, for Dr. Samuel Johnson, the lexicographer, wit and writer, stayed there with his biographer Boswell in 1773. Boswell was unable to give much account of the evening's conversation in his diary, for he and their host got through four bowls of punch.

Some MacKinnons remained in Kintyre. In 1795, Flora MacKinnon and other women, protesting against military recruitment, attacked and disarmed a press gang in Campbeltown. The officer in charge had to be protected from the fury of the women by being barricaded in the shop of a local magistrate. The modern visitor will be received more courteously by the Argyll Tourist Board in MacKinnon House, and directed to the mural of the Crucifixion painted by Alexander MacKinnon in 1887 in a cave on Davaar Island.

MacKinnons suffered along with the other clans during the Clearances. No MacKinnon was a major landowner at that time; these MacKinnons were crofters on other clan lands.

One became a cause celebre. Catherine MacKinnon lived on the coast of Knoydart, on Glengarry land. Glengarry died, leaving his widow, Josephine MacDonnel and their young son in debt. Her factor, Alexander Grant, persuaded her that the remaining crofters must be evicted. Catherine was seventy, lived alone and was ill in bed. She was taken out and put in a ditch while her house was destroyed. Many of the crofters left, but Catherine and some others stayed on.

With winter coming on, the factor's men returned repeatedly to destroy the rough shelters that the remaining crofters had made. The parish priest, Coll MacDonald, wrote of all this to the Glasgow journalist, Donald Ross, who published it in letters to the Northern Ensign. Ross became a one-man aid agency, taking food and blankets to the survivors in an open boat. The letters made a stir, leading to an enquiry by the Fiscal; the end result for the remaining crofters was not an improvement, but their removal.

The crofters of Knoydart were transported to Australia. Over 1,000 crofters, including MacKinnons, from Tiree were sent to Cape Breton in Nova Scotia, where there is still today a high concentration of MacKinnons.

The land rights movement gathered force in the 1880's. In the 'Battle of the Braes', Skye crofters fought the Sheriff of Inverness-shire and 60 men over grazing rights.

Chapter six:

The modern MacKinnons

The chieftaincy was claimed in 1811 by William Alexander MacKinnon, who presented a case to the Lyon Court, the arbiters of heraldic and genealogical matters in Scotland, showing that he descended from Sir Lachlan Mor, whom Charles II knighted, through his second son Donald.

Donald quarrelled with his father, and emigrated to Antigua in about 1680. William was Member of Parliament for various constituencies in Kent from 1819 to 1865, wrote a *History of Civilisation* and was elected Fellow of the Royal Society in 1827. His brother Daniel was colonel and historian of the Coldstream Guards, and was wounded at Waterloo. At least three other MacKinnons achieved general rank in the 19th century.

Meanwhile Sir William MacKinnon founded the British East Africa Company, the trading firm of MacKinnon, MacKenzie & Co., which is still operating in the Far East, and a steamship line. He also promoted an expedition by H.M. Staznley, the explorer who found Livingstone.

MacKinnons who emigrated have also achieved positions of distinction. Major-General Walter MacKinnon, CB, was Chief of the General Staff, New Zealand Army, and his son, Rt. Hon. Donald Charles MacKinnon, became Deputy Prime Minister of New Zealand.

One branch of the family has particular reason to remember and thank Prince Charles. It was he who is said to have imparted the recipe for a whisky liqueur to his friend Captain John MacKinnon. More probably, several branches of the clan were at that time making liqueurs to various recipes (RNI). In 1890, a patent was filed giving the liqueur the name 'Drambuie'. The origin of the name, which may pre-date the patent, is unknown. Perhaps it indicates a connection with Loch Buie in southern Mull. Malcolm MacKinnon started commercial production in

Edinburgh early this century and it is still produced by his grandsons.

There is at the moment no Clan organisation in Britain, but The Clan MacKinnon Society of North America, Inc., is active. For membership information, contact The Clan MacKinnon Society, P.O Box 832, Wilton, CA 95693 USA.

Of all the MacKinnon lands, only Dunakin Castle recently belonged to a MacKinnon; Charles MacKinnon of Dunakin, also descended from the Antigua branch, and hereditary historian of the clan.